SANTA
D0471130

A Dorling Kindersley Book

Project Editor Linda Martin
Art Editor Peter Bailey
Designer Mark Regardsoe
Photography Dave King

First published in Great Britain in 1991 by
Dorling Kindersley Publishers Limited,
9 Henrietta Street, London WC2E 8PS

Reprinted 1993, 1994

Copyright © 1991 *illustrations*
Dorling Kindersley Limited, London
Copyright © 1991 *text* Neil Ardley

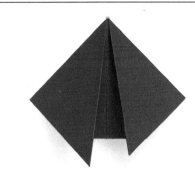

All rights reserved. No part
of this publication may be
reproduced, stored in a retrieval
system, or transmitted in any form
or by any means, electronic,
mechanical, photocopying, recording
or otherwise, without the prior
permission of the copyright owner.

**A CIP catalogue record for this book is available
from the British Library**

ISBN 0-86318-589-4

Reproduced in Hong Kong by Bright Arts
Printed in Belgium by Proost

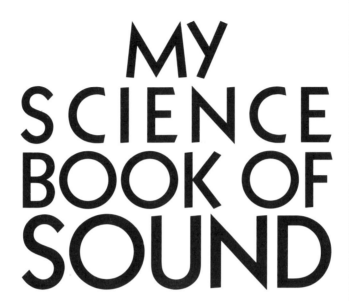

MY SCIENCE BOOK OF SOUND

Written by
Neil Ardley

J 534 ARD
Ardley, Neil.
 My science book of sound
 31994012058811

Dorling Kindersley • London

What is sound?

Sounds are nothing more than tiny shaking movements of the air. You cannot feel these movements, but your ears easily detect them and your brain turns them into sounds that you can recognise. Sounds are all around you. Some are nice, some are horrid! Some are natural, made by people, animals, trees or the wind, and some are made by machines. You use the sounds that you make with your voice to talk to other people. Animals also use sounds as a way of communicating with each other.

Sound signals
We often use sounds as signals. Blowing a whistle in a game can mean "stop" or "go".

Sea songs
Whales in the ocean "sing" to each other. The sound of their song can travel a distance of 800 kilometres!

The speed of sound
The sound of this balloon bursting does not take long to travel through the air. Sound moves through air at 340 metres per second, which is quite fast!

Sound pictures

The picture on this screen shows an unborn baby inside its mother! The picture was made using sounds that are too high-pitched for us to hear. These sounds are called "ultrasound".

Making music

Music is fun. You can make musical sounds with home-made instruments like these.

⚠ This sign means **take care.** You should ask an adult to help you with this step of the experiment.

Be a safe scientist
Follow all the directions carefully and always take care, especially with glass, scissors, matches, candles, and electricity. Never poke anything in your ears, and never put anything in your mouth or eyes. Remember that noise can be irritating. Make sure you do not annoy people by making too much noise!

Squawkers and screechers

Make some strange calls without using your voice. All you need is a piece of plastic, or a straw. With practice, these can give sounds like the cries of wild animals!

You will need:

Drinking straw

Strip of thin plastic

Scissors

1 Hold the strip of plastic tightly between your thumbs and the heels of your hands.

2 Blow hard across the strip. It makes a loud screeching sound!

Try bending your thumbs as you blow.

Keep the end of the straw flat.

Try two or more straws at once. Cut them to different lengths.

1 Press one end of the straw flat. Cut the sides to form a point.

2 Put the pointed end of the straw in your mouth and blow hard. Out comes a weird squawk!

Balloon sounds

Use a balloon to make a loud shrieking noise. You will see how rapid movements, or "vibrations", make sound.

You will need:

Balloon pump

Balloon

1 Pump up the balloon. Hold the neck to stop the air escaping.

2 Grip the neck of the balloon and stretch it. The balloon makes a sound as the air escapes.

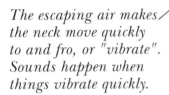

The escaping air makes the neck move quickly to and fro, or "vibrate". Sounds happen when things vibrate quickly.

Tighten or loosen your grip on the balloon to see how many different sounds you can make.

Human sounds
Vocal cords in your throat vibrate and make sounds as the air from your lungs is pushed over them. Your mouth and lips form these sounds into words.

Sound detector

How do we hear the sounds around us? Make a plastic drum and see how it detects the arrival of sound. Your ears detect sound in the same way.

You will need:

Rubber band

Plastic bowl

Saucepan

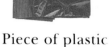
Piece of plastic

Uncooked rice

Scissors

Large spoon

Sticky tape

1 Cut the piece of plastic so that it is bigger than the top of the bowl.

2 Stretch the plastic tightly over the bowl and secure it with a rubber band.

Stretch the plastic as tightly as possible across the bowl.

3 Tape the plastic down to keep it stretched. This is your drum.

4 Sprinkle a few grains of rice on top of the drum.

5 Hold the saucepan near the drum and hit it sharply with the spoon. The grains of rice jump up and down!

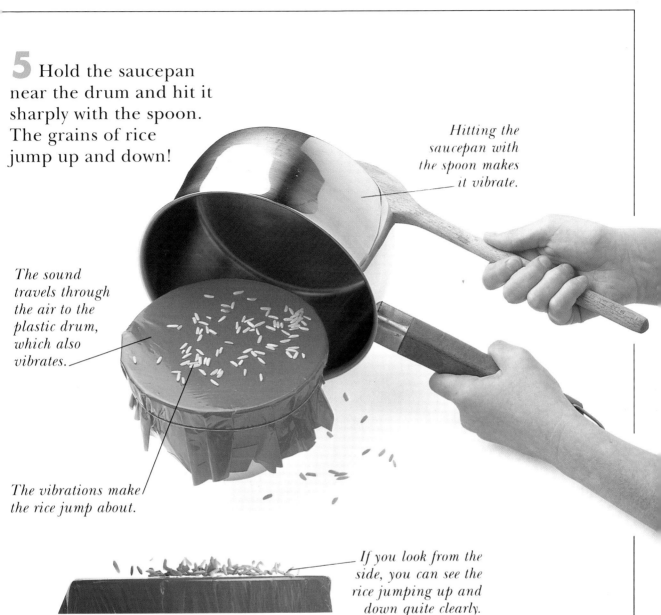

Hitting the saucepan with the spoon makes it vibrate.

The sound travels through the air to the plastic drum, which also vibrates.

The vibrations make the rice jump about.

If you look from the side, you can see the rice jumping up and down quite clearly.

Inside the ear

Inside each of your ears is a thin sheet of skin called the eardrum. Sounds are directed to your eardrum by your outer ear, which is the part you can see. When the sounds reach the eardrum, they make it vibrate, so you hear the sounds.

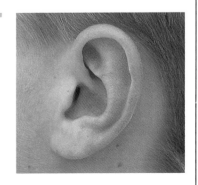

Sound gun

Sounds travel through air by spreading out in invisible waves, rather like ripples on a pond. We call these waves "sound waves". Fire a sound wave at a target and see what happens when the sound reaches it.

You will need:

Thin plastic

Stiff paper

Cardboard tube

Strip of paper

Pencil

Scissors

Rubber band

Sticky tape

1 Use the tube to draw a circle on the piece of paper.

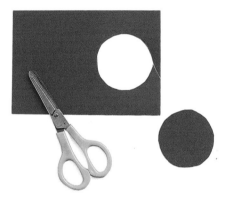

2 Cut out the circle.

3 Make a hole in the centre of the circle with the pencil.

4 Tape the circle firmly to one end of the tube.

5 Fold the plastic over the other end of the tube, and secure it with the rubber band.

6 Fold the paper strip and tape one end to a flat surface so that the other end sticks up.

The tap makes the air inside the tube vibrate and a sound wave travels down the tube.

7 Hold the tube so that the hole points at the top of the paper strip. Sharply tap the other end of the tube.

The air moves to and fro as the sound wave passes, shaking the strip.

The sound wave is pushed through the hole.

Sliding snow
In an avalanche, a mass of snow suddenly slides down a mountain. A loud sound can cause an avalanche. The sound waves disturb the snow and start it moving.

Paper banger

Make a loud bang with a sheet of paper! It will show you how a sudden movement sends a powerful sound wave rushing through the air. You can use your paper banger to surprise and startle your friends. They will all want to make one!

You will need:

Sheet of paper about 30 x 40cm

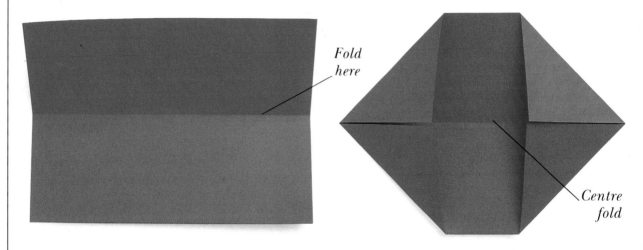

Fold here

Centre fold

1 Fold the longest edges of the paper together, and open it out again.

2 Fold down each of the four corners to the first centre fold.

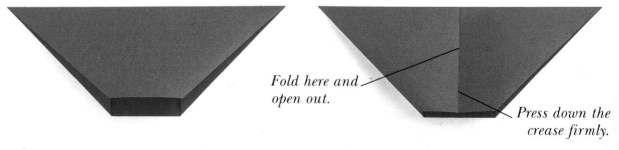

Fold here and open out.

Press down the crease firmly.

3 Fold the paper in half along the first centre fold.

4 Fold the paper in half again and then open it out.

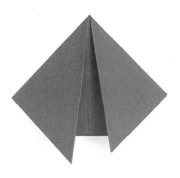

6 Fold the paper back to make a triangle shape. The banger is now ready.

5 Fold down the two top corners.

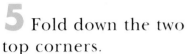

7 Grip the banger firmly by the two top corners. Swish it down sharply with a quick flick of the wrist. A loud bang occurs!

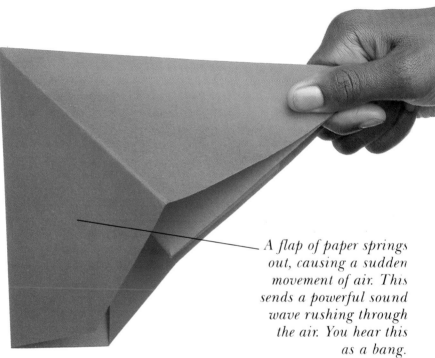

A flap of paper springs out, causing a sudden movement of air. This sends a powerful sound wave rushing through the air. You hear this as a bang.

Thunderclap

In a thunderstorm, a flash of lightning travels from the clouds to the ground at high speed. This causes a powerful sound wave to spread out through the air. We hear a thunderclap when this sound wave reaches our ears.

Talking string

As well as travelling through air, sounds can travel through objects. You can see this by making a simple telephone to talk to your friends with. It will show you how a tight string carries sound even better than air.

You will need:

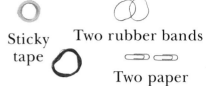

Sticky tape

Two rubber bands

Two pieces of tracing paper

String

Two paper clips

Pencil

Two cardboard tubes

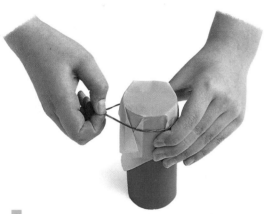

1 Fold a piece of tracing paper over one end of each tube. Fix it with a rubber band.

2 Pull the paper tight and tape it to the tubes.

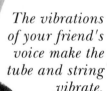

The vibrations of your friend's voice make the tube and string vibrate.

3 Make a small hole in the centre of both pieces of tracing paper.

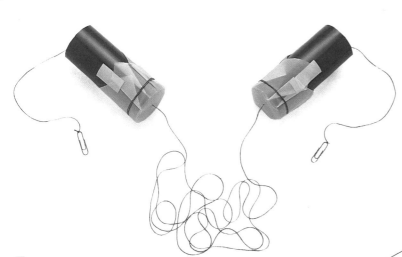

The vibrating string makes your tube vibrate. You hear the vibrations as your friend's voice.

4 Thread the string through both holes. Tie a paperclip to each end to stop the string slipping back through.

The vibrations travel swiftly along the tight string. The sound stops if the string is loose and cannot vibrate.

5 Use the tubes as a simple telephone. Hold one tube to your ear and listen while your friend speaks softly into the other tube.

Prong song
Tapping the prongs of a tuning fork makes a soft musical note. But if you put the handle on a hard surface, the note sings out loudly. The vibrations of the fork travel into the surface, making it vibrate. This makes a much louder sound than the fork alone.

Finding the beat

How can you hear a sound as soft as a heartbeat? Make a simple stethoscope and try it out on a friend. You will see how to make soft sounds loud enough to hear.

You will need:

Scissors

Plastic tubing

Sticky tape

Funnel

1 Put the funnel into the plastic tube and secure it with tape.

Sound waves from the heart collect in the funnel. They travel along the tube to your ear.

Be careful not to stick the tube into your ear.

2 ⚠ Put the funnel against a friend's chest and hold the end of the tube to your ear. You will hear the low thud of their heart beating.

Listening in

The stethoscopes doctors use have two tubes that allow them to use both ears to listen to sounds inside the body. The sounds they hear tell them whether or not parts of the body are working properly.

Loud mouth

How can you make your voice louder without having to shout at the top of your voice? With just a sheet of paper and some sticky tape, you can make a megaphone.

You will need:

Sticky tape

Scissors

Large sheet of paper

1 Roll the paper into a cone.

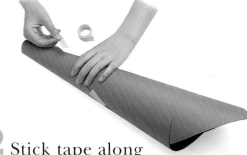

2 Stick tape along the edge of the rolled paper to secure it.

The cone sends the sound waves of your voice forward, and stops them spreading out into the air.

3 Put the cone over your mouth and talk into it. Your voice sounds very loud in front of the cone.

The cone is now an ear trumpet. It collects sounds and directs them to your ear.

4 Now put the cone to your ear. You can hear soft sounds much more easily.

Bouncing sound

Sometimes sound waves hit an object before they reach our ears. When this happens, the sound waves bounce back and we hear the sound as an "echo". This experiment shows you how to bounce sound.

You will need:

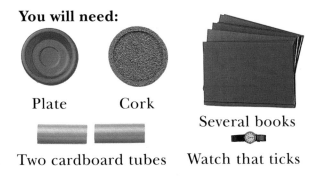

Plate   Cork   Several books

Two cardboard tubes   Watch that ticks

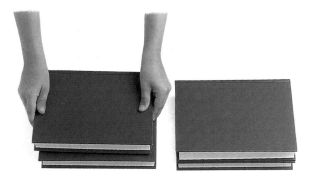

1 Build two piles of books. They must be the same height.

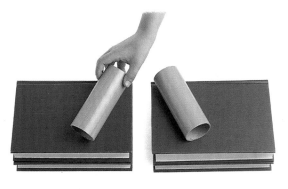

2 Carefully lay the tubes on the books as shown above.

3 Hold the watch to your ear. Listen carefully to make sure you can hear it ticking.

4 Put the watch just inside the end of one tube.

5 Listen at the end of the other tube. You cannot hear the watch. Ask a friend to hold the plate near the far ends of the tubes. Now you can hear the watch.

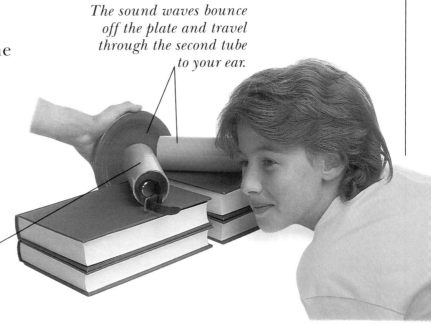

The sound waves bounce off the plate and travel through the second tube to your ear.

Sound waves from the watch travel through the first tube.

The soft cork soaks up the sound waves.

More things to try
Try pieces of wood, metal, or cotton wool. Hear how hard surfaces bounce sounds and soft surfaces do not.

6 Now ask your friend to replace the plate with the cork. This time you cannot hear the watch.

"Seeing" with sound
Bats make high squeaking sounds that bounce off objects in their path. These echoes tell the bats about the size and position of objects. This allows bats to find their way in the dark and catch food, such as flying insects.

Plastic drum

How do musical instruments make sounds? Make a drum to see how to change "pitch", or make the note go higher or lower.

You will need:

Rubber band

Pen

Sheet of plastic

Plastic bowl

1 Fit the plastic over the bowl. Pull the plastic tight and secure it with the rubber band.

2 Grip the plastic firmly to stretch it smoothly across the bowl. Strike it with the pen. Out comes the sound of a drum.

The skin of the drum and the air inside it vibrate to give a booming sound.

Tighten and relax your grip as you play. The note goes up and down. A tighter skin gives a higher pitch.

Talking drum
The cords on this African drum change its pitch. Pressing them while striking the drum raises and lowers the note and produces sounds similar to an African language!

Simple shakers

Many percussion instruments produce various kinds of noises as you beat or shake them. Make some shakers. You can use them to play a lively rhythm for dancing.

You will need:

Plastic bottle

Scissors

Paperclips

Coloured sticky tape

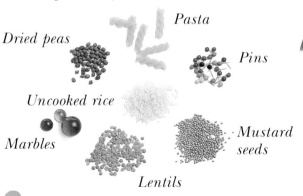

Make sure the bottle is dry inside.

1 Put a few paper clips into the bottle. Screw on the cap firmly.

Pasta

Dried peas

Pins

Uncooked rice

Marbles

Mustard seeds

Lentils

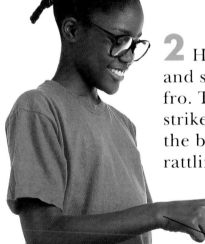

2 Hold the bottle and shake it to and fro. The paperclips strike the sides of the bottle to give a rattling sound.

Shake with short flicks of the wrist.

3 Collect other small objects and make more shakers with them. They all give different sounds.

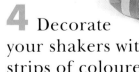

4 Decorate your shakers with strips of coloured tape.

Rubber guitar

Make music with some rubber bands! Stretch the bands across a tin and pluck them. Out will come the sound of a guitar. This experiment will help you understand how "string" instruments work.

You will need:

Three colouring pens

Baking tin

Rubber bands of varying thickness

1 Stretch the rubber bands lengthways across the tin.

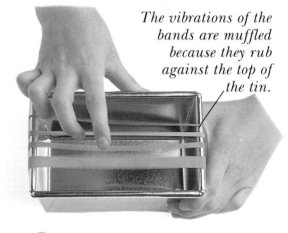

The vibrations of the bands are muffled because they rub against the top of the tin.

2 Pluck the bands to hear what sort of sound they make. It is rather dull!

The pens hold the rubber bands above the tin.

3 Now put a pen underneath the rubber bands at each end of the tin.

4 Pluck the bands again. The sound is much clearer than it was before.

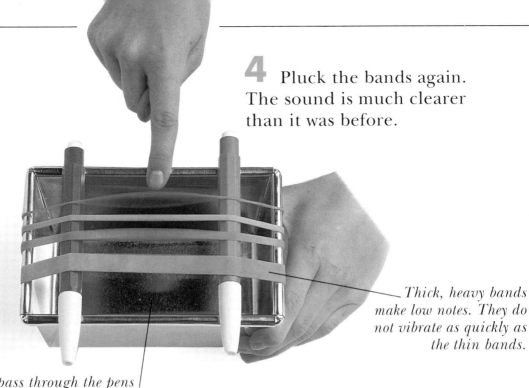

Thick, heavy bands make low notes. They do not vibrate as quickly as the thin bands.

Vibrations pass through the pens to the tin. Most of the sound comes from the tin as it vibrates.

5 Press the third pen on the bands. Slide it up and down as you pluck the bands. The pitch of the notes changes.

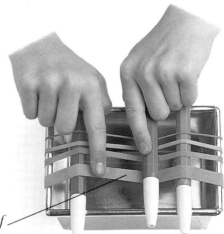

The notes get higher as you shorten the vibrating part of each band.

String sounds
Guitar players press the strings with one hand and pluck them with the other. Pressing the strings changes the notes by making the vibrating parts shorter or longer.

Bottle pipes

You can also make your own music with a few bottles and a little water. You will see and hear how different amounts of air can vibrate to give quite different sounds.

You will need:

Food colouring or ink

Jug of water

Narrow-necked glass bottles

1 Set out the bottles in a line. You will need six or more bottles to make a tune.

2 Pour a different amount of water into each bottle.

Gradually change the level of water in each bottle.

3 You can colour the water to make the levels easier to see, and to make the bottles look pretty!

4 Blow gently across the top of each bottle. Each one makes a different musical note. You can try changing the water levels to get notes that make a tune.

Blowing across the top of the bottle makes the air inside vibrate. Short air spaces vibrate more quickly than long air spaces.

A long column of air makes a low note.

A short column of air gives a high note.

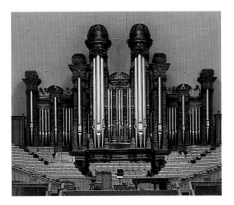

Pipe organ
Each pipe in this huge organ sounds one note. When the organ is played, air is blown across holes at the base of each pipe, causing the column of air in the pipe to vibrate and produce a note. Together, these notes form music.

Music with holes

"Woodwind" instruments, such as the flute, clarinet, and oboe, are pipes with holes in them. You can make your own wood-wind instrument from a cardboard tube and produce several notes from just one pipe.

You will need:

Cardboard tube

Drinking straw

Tracing paper

Pencil

Scissors

Sticky tape

1 Press one end of the straw flat. Cut the sides to make a point.

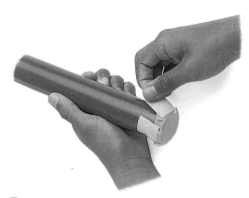

2 Fold the tracing paper over one end of the tube and secure it with sticky tape.

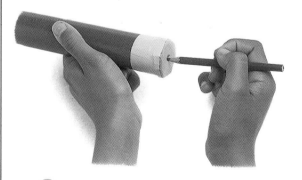

3 Using the pencil, make a small hole in the centre of the tracing paper.

4 Carefully push the round end of the straw through the hole.

The straw vibrates and sets the air in the tube vibrating as far as the first hole.

5 With the pencil, make six holes along the length of the tube.

6 Cover the holes with your fingers and blow. By moving your fingers on and off the holes, you can change the pitch of the note.

The longer the column of air, the lower the note is.

Bags of sound
To play the bagpipes, the player squeezes the bag, which sends air rushing into the pipes. The pipe with holes, the "chanter", plays a tune. The other pipes each sound one note only.

Picture credits
(Abbreviation key: B=below, C=centre, L=left, R=right, T=top)

Catherine Ashmore: 25BL; Clive Barda: 9BL; Dorling Kindersley: 22BL; Pete Gardner: 6BL, 6BR, 7CL, 11BR, 17BR; Robert Harding Picture Library: 13BL; The Image Bank: 15BL; Dave King: 6TL; NHPA/Trureo Nakamuta: 6CR; Stephen Dalton: 21BR; Science Photo Library/ Alexander Tsiaras: 7TL; Chris Priest & Mark Clarke: 18BL; Scottish Tourist Board: 29CL; Zefa: 27BL.

Picture research Paula Cassidy and Rupert Thomas

Production Louise Barratt

Dorling Kindersley would like to thank Claire Gillard for editorial assistance; Mrs Bradbury, the staff and children of Allfarthing Junior School, Wandsworth, especially Idris Anjary, Melanie Best, Benny Grebot, Miriam Habtesellasse, Alistair Lambert, Lucy Martin, Paul Nolan, Dorothy Opong, Alan Penfold, Ben Saunders, David Tross and Alice Watling; Tom Armstrong, Michael Brown, Damien Francis, Stacey Higgs, Mela Macgregor, Katie Martin, Susanna Scott, Natasha Shepherd and Victoria Watling.